THE POSI GROUNDHOG

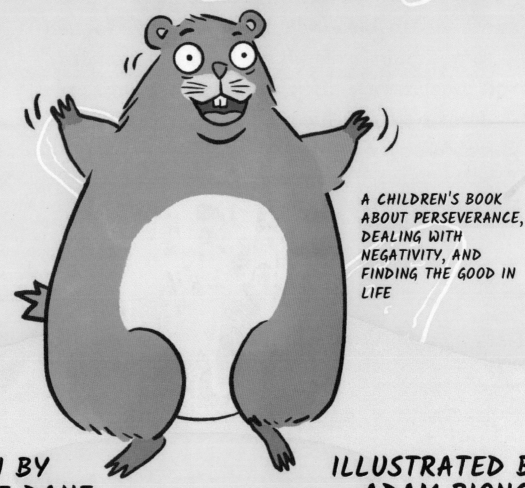

A CHILDREN'S BOOK ABOUT PERSEVERANCE, DEALING WITH NEGATIVITY, AND FINDING THE GOOD IN LIFE

WRITTEN BY CHARLOTTE DANE

ILLUSTRATED BY ADAM RIONG

THE POSITIVE GROUNDHOG

If there is one thing everyone knew about Groundhog, it was that he was the most positive animal they had ever met.

It was like he didn't know what a frown was.
He always chose to see the good in a situation.
He would say, "Nothing is ever that bad!"

Groundhog just thought of his favorite bedtime stories: "Heroes always have to overcome a challenge! This is just my turn."

However, Groundhog wasn't always like this. In fact, there was a time when even something tiny would make Groundhog think that the world was ending. Instead of being excited about things, he was just negative and scared.

One time, Groundhog was trying to learn how to ride a bicycle.

He fell so hard the first time he got on!
He ran home and declared that he would only
walk for the rest of his life!

Another time, Groundhog gave a class presentation on owls.

Even if Groundhog did something great, like when he won a ribbon for his math skills, he would always find a way to feel bad about it.

And boy, no one likes to hang out with a dark and stormy cloud!

One day, Groundhog's friend Fox noticed and came over to talk to him. Fox asked him why he seemed upset all the time.

Groundhog said, "Whenever something bad happens, I think 10 more bad things will follow!" As soon as he said this, Fox knew exactly how to help his friend.

Fox took Groundhog to a cookie factory the next weekend.

Groundhog's favorite cookie was chocolate chip, while Fox's was double chocolate chip.

The next day at school, Groundhog broke his pencil again. He took a deep breath and thought of the Cookie Rule.

Breaking his pencil was a bad cookie, but there are so many wonderful chocolate chip cookies just waiting for him.

He was able to stay positive and calmly get another pencil - a new one that was his favorite color, blue! He was successful!

The next week, Groundhog tripped and fell into a big puddle while he was wearing all white.

The Cookie Rule to the rescue! 10 bad minutes doesn't have to affect the rest of the 1430 minutes. Groundhog got to leave school early and his mother treated him to ice cream and pizza.

Groundhog realized a few things. Feeling positive was actually his choice. Bad things don't mean that other bad things will happen. You can always find the good in a situation.

FOR MORE, VISIT
BIGBARNPRESS.COM

Printed in Great Britain
by Amazon